An Excellent Spirit: Living Life Wholly Unto God

Chris A. Legebow

DEDICATION

I thank God for the Macchiavello family for living their lives of excellence towards God in their career, ministry and private lives. I thank God for the Christian preachers and teachers who have especially ministered to me because of their excellence: Kenneth and Gloria Copeland, Joyce Meyer, Marilyn Hickey, Benny Hinn and so many others…

Chris Legebow

CONTENTS

ACKNOWLEDGMENTS

All Scripture taken from Bible Gateway. com
Modern English Version (MEV)

1. AN EXCELLENT SPIRIT

Daniel 1: 3 The king spoke to Ashpenaz the master of his officials that he should bring some of the sons of Israel and some of the king's descendants and some of the nobles, 4 youths in whom was no blemish, who were handsome and skillful in every branch of wisdom and gifted with understanding and discerning knowledge, and such as had ability in them to serve in the king's palace, and whom they might teach the learning and the language of the Chaldeans. 5 The king appointed them a daily provision of the king's food and of the wine which he drank. They were to be educated for three years, that at the end of it they might serve before the king.

King Nebuchadnezzar

The verse above begins with captives of Israel who are brought to Babylon as slaves. Nebuchadnezzar, the king of Babylon, took for himself the spoils of Israel. He did not kill all people. In fact, he searched for those who were intelligent and excellent and who could perhaps serve him to be brought and raised in in the Palace. This shows that he knew and valued the elite of Israel. He wanted what was best. He wasn't going to let them be free but thought perhaps they might be worth training and raising as Babylonians to serve him.

He only takes what is best, the cream of the crop as we would say, those who were elite. The king gives them special treatment. They are brought to live in the Palace although they are slaves. They are taught the language and culture of Babylon. They are groomed to be advisors to the king. Not too many would consider taking one's enemies captives to be trained to serve and advise him. There are many kings who would have killed all of these types of people in order to eradicate the race of people they had captured.

Daniel 1: 6 Now among them were of the sons of Judah: Daniel, Hananiah, Mishael, and Azariah, 7 to whom the commander of the officials gave names. And he gave to Daniel the name of Belteshazzar; to Hananiah, Shadrach; to Mishael, Meshach; and to Azariah, Abednego.
8 But Daniel purposed in his heart that he would not defile himself with the

portion of the king's food, nor with the wine which he drank. Therefore he requested of the master of the officials that he might not defile himself.

Daniel Purposed in his Heart

First, they were given Babylonian names. Next, they were taught the language and culture of their captors. Daniel's commitment to God was so strong that even in his captivity, he desired to serve and honour God. Teen age boys can be inspired for tremendous good because they are strong and passionate; they could also go to the other extreme if they were not serving the LORD. Daniel purposed in his heart – he made a willful decision to serve God. His faith encouraged his friends to join him. They determined to remember God and honour Him.

Daniel 1: 9 Now God had brought Daniel into favor and compassion with the master of the officials. 10 The master of the officials said to Daniel, "I fear my lord the king who has appointed your food and your drink. For why should he see your faces worse-looking than the youths who are your age? Then you would endanger my head before the king."

God had a special anointing on Daniel that was his faith and that also gave him favour with the captain of the guard.

The Israelis Were to be Given Babylon's Best

Their food would have consisted of Babylon's finest. Strangled animals including pork, cooked in blood and wine offered to their pagan gods would have been offered to them. Partaking of this type of food was completely against the Levitical laws given to Moses by God. God forbid his people to eat or drink blood. Pork was also forbidden. They should serve no other God except Jehovah. That meant they could not take any food or drink that had been dedicated to a pagan god. This food and drink would be considered an abomination to God.

The guard official spoke openly and explained to Daniel that if they did not eat the special food and drink and they were to appear ill or not strong, he could lose his life. He literally feared for his life because his job was to make of all these youths the best candidates to be advisors to the king. They should be strong and superior to most people. He believed if they did not eat the bloody meat (my wording), they would not be strong. He didn't know any other way. Because they were slaves there was no respect for their religion or their customs – there was a desire to use their best qualities and make of them Babylonians. God's favour was on them so strong that the guard listened to their request and granted it to them.

Daniel Gets an Inspiration; I do Believe God Gave him this Wisdom.

Daniel 1: 11 Then Daniel said to the steward, whom the master of the officials had set over Daniel, Hananiah, Mishael, and Azariah, 12 "Please test your servants for ten days, and let them give us vegetables to eat and water to drink. 13 Then let our countenances be looked upon before you, and the countenance of the youths who eat of the portion of the king's food. And as you see, deal with your servants." 14 So he consented to them in this matter and tested them for ten days.

Daniel says they would only eat vegetables and fruit and drink water. In this way, they would be honouring God and he believed they would be healthy and that God would honour their faith. If they were to be unhealthy after the week had passed, they would agree to the bloody meat diet. Daniel believed they would be healthy with vegetables and fruit and water. And it was true. They stayed strong in their health and spirit even though they did not have meat or wine. Ashpenaz, the captain of the guard, knew there was something special about these Israelis and let them have the request of their diet. The youth were knowledgeable; they were excellent in their spirit and wise and quick to learn.

Daniel 1: 17 As for these four youths, God gave them knowledge and skill in every branch of learning and wisdom. And Daniel had understanding in all kinds of visions and dreams.

I am sure that Daniel and his friends were praying. This diet of Daniel and his friends is a popular fast people go on for religious purposes – the Daniel fast. Daniel and his friends kept the laws of God and God prospered them, even though they were slaves. It does not take away from the fact that they were taken from all the comforts they knew and loved in Israel. They were slaves, but their treatment was special because God's anointing or presence was upon them inspiring them to live lives of integrity. The scripture says their countenance stayed strong. It is a word that means more than outward appearance but their appearance and their good spirits made them appear attractive and strong. The scripture says that they appeared healthier than all of the other people.

They had knowledge and skill superior to the others in all kinds of learning. That means the language, the history, the culture, the traditions, the architecture and technology. Babylon was known to be a rich and mature culture. It had special arts and was known for its skill in the hanging gardens of Babylon; they built many notable structures and were admired for its advanced society. They were a complex society. They were civilized.

Daniel's interpretation of dreams was also a strong gifting. Not only was he wise and intelligent and excellent in every way, he was also given the interpretation of King Nebuchadnezzar's dream. It was an impossible task he was given as the king demanded the wise men tell him his dream and the interpretation of it. None of the other wise men were able to do it because only God Himself knows what a man dreams and what the dream means.

Daniel 2: 47 The king answered Daniel and said, "Truly your God is a God of gods, and a Lord of kings, and a revealer of secrets, since you could reveal this secret."

Daniel Lion's Den

With new the new king Darius as ruler, those who hated Daniel and the Israelis sought ways to get rid of Daniel. They schemed to cause his death. Daniel was living his life so excellently that the only area of potential weakness any one could find in him was his faith in Jehovah God.

Daniel 6: 4 Then the presidents and officials sought to find occasion against Daniel concerning the kingdom, but they could find no occasion or fault because he was faithful; nor was there any error or fault found in him. 5 Then these men said, "We shall not find any occasion against this Daniel, unless we find it against him concerning the law of his God."

The corrupt wise men approached the king appealing to his sense of pride. They suggested a decree or law that forbid anyone from praying to any other God than the king. This is the same evil that tried to destroy Hananiah, Azariah and Mishael. If they could get the Israelis to worship the king of Babylon instead of God they would win. If the Israeli would not bow to the king, they would. The enemies of the Israeli would win. After the king agrees to this suggestion, he is almost immediately confronted by those evil wise men who accused Daniel of praying to Jehovah. Daniel did not hide his faith. He served God faithfully since his youth and continued to pray and praise God.

Daniel 6: 13 Then they answered and said before the king, "That Daniel, who is of the sons of the captivity of Judah, does not regard you, O king, or the decree that you have signed, but makes his petition three times a day." 14 Then the king, when he heard these words, was sorely displeased with himself and set his heart on Daniel to deliver him. And he labored until sunset to deliver him.

The king realized that he had been tricked into the decree by the scheming wise men who hated Daniel. He had agreed that his own law could not be altered or changed. He had to keep his own rule even though it meant the certain death of Daniel. The king had Daniel thrown into the lion's den. Lions were kept and used as a horrible way to kill the enemies of the king. Please note that the king earnestly cared for Daniel and said kind words to him even upon executing the decree.

Daniel 6: 16 Then the king commanded, and they brought Daniel and cast him into the den of lions. Now the king spoke and said to Daniel, "Your God whom you serve continually, He will deliver you."

The scripture says it bothered the king so much that he fasted and prayed because of Daniel. It is obvious that Daniel was a faithful servant to this king as well. Early the next day, Darius went to the lion's den. His words show that Daniel's faith to Jehovah had been a witness to this king also because he says the following:

Daniel 6: And the king spoke and said to Daniel, "Daniel, servant of the living God, has your God whom you serve continually been able to deliver you from the lions?"

It was as though he were expecting a response. The king had some forth of faith shown through his actions and also his words.

Daniel is not bitter or angry. He greets the king as to a friend and gives an honest reply of what occurred during the night.

Daniel 6: 21 Then Daniel said to the king, "O king, live forever! 22 My God has sent His angel and has shut the lions' mouths so that they have not hurt me, because innocence was found in me before Him; and also before you, O king, I have done no harm."

Even though this king sentenced him to be thrown in the Lion's den, Daniel knew the true enemy was the enemy of God. He did not view the king as the enemy because he realizes the king was tricked into doing it. Daniel admits he was innocent of any crime against the king and has only served him faithfully. Those evil wise men were sentenced to be thrown to the lions because of their evil plot against Daniel. The king made a new, wise decree regarding Daniel and the Israelis.

Daniel 6: 25 Then King Darius wrote:

To all peoples, nations, and languages that dwell in all the earth:
"Peace be multiplied unto you.
 26 "I make a decree that in every dominion of my kingdom men are to
fear and tremble before the God of Daniel.
"For He is the living God,
    enduring forever;
His kingdom shall never be destroyed,
    and His dominion shall be forever.
27 He delivers and rescues,
    and He works signs and wonders
    in heaven and on earth,
who has delivered Daniel
from the power of the lions."

Darius, like Nebuchadnezzar, was also a living witness of the God of
Daniel. His decree similar to that of Nebuchadnezzar speaks of the God of
Israel as being the one true God. Daniel's heart was pure. He was not in any
way injured. He was affirmed by God as a servant of God by his
deliverance out of the lion's den. The ability to forgive someone who has
sentenced you to death is tremendous. I'm not sure how often this part of
the story is emphasized but most people would have believed the king to be
guilty of a crime. Daniel's true desire to serve Jehovah God and the king
was proven by his response to the king.

Dreams and Visons of Daniel

A new king Belshazzar became the ruler of the territory. Daniel was
given a special dream by God. There were four beasts that Daniel saw.
Daniel 7: 2- 13 discusses the dream. Daniel knew it wasn't a normal dream.
He knew it was a dream from God but He didn't understand it. He knew
that he recognized God "The ancient od Days" and the Messiah: the son of
man". He knew it was a symbolic dream but did not have the interpretation
of it. Please notice, this same Daniel had interpreted Nebuchadnezzar's
dream. It wasn't a natural ability that Daniel possessed but interpretation of
dreams can only come through God. Daniel was not given the meaning of
the dream; he only knew God was speaking to him through the dream. The
dream was a view into the future of what would happen on earth. He saw
kingdom's rise and fall. He saw finally the kingdom of God. He is given
more symbolic dreams of the future that overwhelm him and cause him to
pray because he does not know what the dreams mean (Daniel 8). Daniel
knows that only God could reveal such dreams so he prays for the

interpretation. The messenger angel Gabriel is sent to help Daniel understand the dreams.

Gabriel explains the dreams are of the end of days. Often these chapters regarding Daniel's dreams and visions are used with the book of Revelation to help people understand what will happen before Jesus returns to earth. Daniel is instructed by the angel to keep these things to himself because it is not to occur until the distant future.

Daniel 8: 26 "And the vision of the evenings and the mornings, which was told, is true. Therefore shut up the vision, for it deals with many days in the future."

Even though the angel explains these things are in the future, even though an angel appears to him to give him meaning, even though Daniel knows it is from God. It causes him to feel weak and overwhelmed by what he has seen. The truths of divine providence and prophetic dreaming can be overwhelming to a human being. Please know that Daniel was a chosen vessel for God to give the visions of the end of days on the earth.

Prophetic People can be Overwhelmed by Visions and Dreams

Sometimes being of an excellent spirit, prophetic people will be overwhelmed by the presence of God and the revelations from God. Even though we are spiritual, the knowledge of God is completely over whelming to us should God show it to us. It is possible for God to show us things that completely overwhelm us. If God gives you information you do not understand in a dream or vision, pray about it. The first thing to do is to go to the God who gave you the dream or vision. Next ask God for the interpretation. Pray and ask God what you should do with the information. God may send an angel to you or a person who will help to explain it.

There is an aspect of intercessory prayer and prophecy that can completely overwhelm a servant of God – even an excellent person of God – because he or she is a human being. The things of the Holy Spirit are beyond all natural understanding. There are people, prophets who may be given special visions and dreams and prophecies that are not for the immediate future but are to happen later in life. God entrusts these truths to them because He knows they will obey him. It is possible that you may receive a message of God that is not for you only but for many people or all people, but not during your lifetime.

Daniel is so overwhelmed by the visions and dreams that he prays and fasts seeking God and praying repentance for Israel. He confesses his sins and his people's sins and prays for Israel. Please know his being overwhelmed by the future causes him to take strong action in the present by praying and fasting. He does the only thing he knows he must do – pray for mercy. This is the response we should have if we receive information from God that we do not understand. Only God knows what He has imparted and only God knows the correct interpretation of it.

The angel Gabriel who had seen in the dream/vision came to him (Daniel 9) and spoke with him and comforted him by explaining the dreams and visions once more. God honoured Daniel's faith. God showed mercy on Daniel by sending Gabriel to comfort him and explain things to him even though it was overwhelming. Once more Daniel is overwhelmed by dreams of the future (Daniel 10). He fasted and prayed and sought and answer from God for three weeks. Daniel alone was given the vision. Those with Daniel were overcome by fear – something strange was occurring and they ran away from it. Daniel was trembling and completely overcome. Please see that Daniel lived his life as holy as he could. He was "greatly beloved" by God as the angel greats him. Daniel is given understanding of the real enemy – demonic spirits that tried to block the angel Gabriel from coming to help Daniel understand the interpretation of the dreams and visions.

Not all prophets get visions of the end of life on earth as we know it. Not many prophets are given God's perspective on things on earth that will occur on a global scale. It causes Daniel to pray and intercede for himself and for Israel and for God's mercy. Pray that your heart will remain pure that God might entrust the riches of heaven to you so that you can be a faithful witness for God on the earth. Whatever revelation you do get, pray that God will show you what to do with it, how to pray, whom to share with etc. What is born of the Holy Spirit can only be directed best by the Holy Spirit.

Prayer

O God use me with wisdom beyond all natural understanding so I might be able to help others by speaking inspired words to bring them to you. Amen

2 SPIRITUAL GIFTINGS

Daniel had special spiritual wisdom from God so that he had knowledge of all dreams and visons. God gave him the interpretation of them. Not only did they have natural understanding but supernatural understanding. Clearly, God`s favour was upon them. Knowing dreams and visions is not a natural thing. It is studied in Psychology but these are theories about them not knowledge. Different people believe certain symbols are sexual; some believe they are archetypal. Psychology is not knowing – it is only about theories of what might be true. Daniel had supernatural knowledge given to him by God so that he knew certainly and could interpret the meaning of dreams. We might call this a prophetic type of gifting. Verse 20 informs us that the wisdom on the Israelis was much superior to any of the other wise men.

Only God can give the true interpretation of dreams. God can and does give dreams to people to warn them, to instruct them, to lead the, etc. The same God that gives the dream and also give the interpretation. This is divine knowledge. God doesn`t impart it to just anyone. He gives it to those who consecrate themselves unto Him completely. He doesn`t just give extraordinary wisdom or knowledge to all people. He gives it to those who can give Him glory by using it to help others.

God wants to share His heart with you. God wants to use you in spiritual gifts. Should you want to serve God, He will anoint you with special giftings that you can use to bring God glory. It is not for entertainment but it is for God`s glory. These gifts are mentioned throughout the scriptures but are expressed in the New Testament as this list.

1 Corinthians 12: 7 But the manifestation of the Spirit is given to everyone for the common good. 8 To one is given by the Spirit the word of wisdom, to another the word of knowledge by the same Spirit, 9 to another faith by the same Spirit, to another gifts of healings by the same Spirit, 10 to another the working of miracles, to another prophecy, to another discerning of spirits, to another various kinds of tongues, and to another the interpretation of tongues. 11 But that one and very same Spirit works all these, dividing to each one individually as He will.

Giftings

God empowers His people with spiritual gifts so that they might be witness for God. The giftings are to be used with the unction of the Holy Spirit, for the glory of God. I believe teenagers and twenty somethings and thirty somethings who are keen for God are unstoppable. They will hold on to their faith with boldness and can be a mighty Spiritual influence throughout their generation. Just as God used Daniel and his friends, anointing or covering them with special favour, God can use youth today to impact the world with the Light of Christ's good news of Salvation. God gives to faithful youth a boldness that cannot be denied. They will live for God or die for Him. They are passionate. God gave special wisdom and knowledge to be as leaders in their roles in Babylon. They were treated kindly and respected for wisdom and knowledge. They were of an excellent Spirit – without compromise.

The other wise men in Babylon chosen to give wise counsel to the king of Babylon were diviners and astrologers. They used pagan practices such as mixing animal organs and blood to foretell the future. They were gazing on the stars and foretelling the future. They were not following God. They were doing things according to their pagan gods. God forbids these types of pagan practices because wants us to come to Him for revelation and wisdom. I am saying there are other ways of getting information rather than going to God. There may be some truth in what people discover using sorcery – but they are not going to God as their source; this is a direct sin against God who commands that we do not go to any other gods
(Deuteronomy 5: 7). People who go to any one but God are putting their faith in pagan gods which are really demons.

God is the Only Source

I caution you to be careful that you only go to the true source of wisdom and knowledge and that is Jehovah God. He revealed Himself in human form as the Son of God the LORD Jesus Christ. There is only one right way to serve and honour God. That is by going to God Himself not trying to use witchcraft or zodiac knowledge. It is a direct sin against the first commandment and the demons who give such information to people put their hooks into the person and may use those people. Please understand, the demons are not trying to give us knowledge to help us. They hate us and would destroy us. If they give any truth, it is twisted and will lead to death. It may be physical death; it certainly leads to spiritual death and separation from God.

John 14: 6 Jesus said to him, "I am the way, the truth, and the life. No one comes to the Father except through Me.

People who go to any other source but God are directly going against God and His ways. God calls these things an abomination to Him. Among the wise men of Babylon, the king's counsellors, only Daniel and his friends were serving Jehovah God. God's favour was on them because they worshipped God in spite of their situation. They prayed and only served God. Please realize the other people were worshipping false gods. It could have been easy for them to go along with the crowd and do what everyone else was doing. After Nebuchadnezzar is given the meaning of his dream by the Spirit of God using Daniel, Nebuchadnezzar builds the image he dreamed about and caused all the kingdom to bow down and worship it. Instead of serving the God who gave the interpretation of the dream, he gets prideful. Whatever the king decreed was what the people did or they were killed.

Daniel 3: 4 Then a herald cried aloud: "To you it is commanded, O peoples, nations, and languages, 5 that at the time you hear the sound of the cornet, flute, harp, sackbut, psaltery, dulcimer, and all kinds of music, you should fall down and worship the golden image that Nebuchadnezzar the king has set up. 6 And whoever does not fall down and worship shall the same hour be cast into the midst of a burning fiery furnace."

Shadrach, Meshach and Abednego

Please see it was clearly indicated to them the penalty for disobedience. The other wise men hated Daniel and Hananiah , Azariah, and Mishael. Not all people are going to like you should you worship God and serve Him wholly. Their enemies complained to the king hoping that would be the end of the Israelis.

Daniel 3: 8 Therefore at that time certain Chaldeans came near and accused the Jews. 9 They spoke and said to King Nebuchadnezzar, "O king, live forever. 10 You, O king, have made a decree, that every man who hears the sound of the cornet, flute, harp, sackbut, psaltery, and dulcimer, and all kinds of music should fall down and worship the golden image. 11 And whoever does not fall down and worship should be cast into the midst of a burning fiery furnace. 12 There are certain Jews whom you have set over the affairs of the province of Babylon: Shadrach, Meshach, and Abednego. These men, O king, have not regarded you. They do not serve your gods or worship the golden image which you have set up."

If you know the story, you know the king questions them and gives them a chance to bow to the statue to spare their lives. He wanted his will to be enforced. Please notice he had no respect for God. They understood it could mean their death but they proclaimed the following:

Daniel 3: 16 Shadrach, Meshach, and Abednego answered and said to the king, "O Nebuchadnezzar, we do not need to give you an answer in this matter. 17 If it be so, our God whom we serve is able to deliver us from the burning fiery furnace, and He will deliver us out of your hand, O king. 18 But even if He does not, be it known to you, O king, that we will not serve your gods, nor worship the golden image which you have set up."

Pride in King Nebuchadnezzar

That king was so angry that they refused to bow to his image that he made a false god, he demand the oven be heated 7X hotter than usual. The Israelis were tied up with ropes and thrown into the furnace. The temperature was so hot that the guards throwing the Israelis in died. All of this was done with Nebuchadnezzar watching. He was amazed at the result. God saw their faith and honoured it. He also wanted to show His glory. An appearance of an extra person in the furnace walking around with the Israelis was seen. They were no longer tied. They were walking around in the oven so hot that it would kill anyone near it.

It is a direct witness to all the people who were watching the situation but it is especially a proof to Nebuchadnezzar that these Israelis were serving the only true God. He realizes his error by his words:

Daniel 3: 26 Then Nebuchadnezzar came near to the mouth of the burning fiery furnace, and spoke, and said, "Shadrach, Meshach, and Abednego, you servants of the Most High God, come out and come here!"

28 Then Nebuchadnezzar spoke and said, "Blessed be the God of Shadrach, Meshach, and Abednego, who has sent His angel and delivered His servants who trusted in Him. They have defied the king's word, and yielded their bodies, that they might not serve nor worship any god, except their own God. 29 Therefore I make a decree that every people, nation, and language which speaks anything amiss against the God of Shadrach, Meshach, and Abednego shall be cut in pieces, and their houses shall be made a dunghill, because there is no other God who can deliver in this way."

Please read the scripture with a sense of awe. God used the horrible situation to reach towards Nebuchadnezzar once more. God wanted in some way to show mercy to this king. Yes, God saved his servants. That is miraculous and awesome; He could have done it in so many other ways, but God also so impressed the king, who was an idol worshipper, with miraculous proof that God was real that the king confessed before the people that Shadrach, Meshach and Abednego worshipped the only true God. He made a decree or law that no one could come against them or their God. It was a direct reversal or his prideful law that forced people to bow to the idol. He promoted the Israeli and what was meant by their enemies to destroy them ended up promoting them to a higher position and also giving the King knowledge of the true and living God.

God Wants to use you in the Gifts of the Holy Spirit

God created us to be in close relationship with Him. We are to go to God for wisdom and discernment and knowledge. God forbids us to go any other way. If we truly love God, we will go God`s way. It means we humbly admit we need God. Often God quickens a scripture to you. Sometimes, he may speak words to you on the inside of your spirit. Please do not believe the lie that God wants you ignorant. God can give you wisdom, knowledge and understanding that surpasses all types of earthly wisdom.

1 Corinthians 1: 25 For the foolishness of God is wiser than men, and the weakness of God is stronger than men.

The Spiritual gifts are the primary way God uses us to witness to people or share Christ with them. They are all from the Holy Spirit. They are all for the glory of God. I discuss these gifts in much detail in the book on the gifts of the Holy Spirit but want to give a brief description of them here in case they are new to you. Please do further reading on these gifts as they are vital to a person serving God. Sometimes 3 or 4 are most prominent giftings but because Jesus lives on the inside of you, there is some aspect of the gifting in your spirit.

Words of Wisdom

As soon as you become a Christian, the Holy Spirit living on the inside of you begins to teach you about God through His Word the Bible and through teaching and preaching and through living on the inside of you throughout the day. God's desire is to use you in the gifts of the Holy Spirit. Words of wisdom are special insights that only God can give because He knows all things. He can give us the words to speak that are exactly what solves a problem or a situation. He can use whatever earthly education you have and cause you to understand it with illumination from the Spirit so that it is the answer you need.

Words of knowledge

Words of knowledge are when God reveals to you secrets of someone's life so you can either pray for them or share Christ with them or in some way reconcile that person to God. Interpretation of dreams often comes to prophetic people or people who are used by God in the gift of prophecy. Don't assume they are for everybody else except you. If you have a certain dream that you believe is special, pray and ask God to give you the meaning.

Interpretation of dreams

Something important I would have done differently had I known about it is praying more about the dreams God gave me and asking Him for the meaning and asking Him how to pray about it and also what I should do. I have realized that the dreams themselves were only a conversation starter and I should have talked to God more to help me to understand what dreams I had been given. Getting the dream isn't the answer – it is either to prompt you to pray or to help someone etc. Only God knows the reason. Seeking Him about it is most important.

Discerning of Spirits

Discerning of spirits is knowing the Holy Spirit's presence and recognizing an evil presence. This gift is usually given to warn us and also to give us the joy of experiencing God's presence. The gifts reside in every born again servant of God. The baptism of the Holy Spirit empowers us to use these gifts so more people can be saved. God wants to use those who give their lives to god wholly.

Gift of Faith

The gift of faith is necessary for us to come to God. If we do not believe that God loves us and that Jesus died for us to be saved, we cannot become Christians. Please see that it was God drawing you to Himself. God's love compelled us to repent and receive Him as Saviour. There are special reasons people get the gift of faith – it is usually because they need a miracle. It is God empowered a believer to have supernatural faith to believe for something beyond all human ability. It could be healing from a terminal illness. It could be praying for a huge amount to money.

My former pastor, believed God would give him the land he saw even though they [the church] did not have enough money. They believed; they confessed the word – speaking God will give us the ground to build a church on. They walked around the new land site claiming it for God to build their church. They did all they could humanly do and believed for a miracle of finances. Almost to the last minute, the money came in and they purchased the land where a huge sanctuary sits today.

The Gifts of Healing

The gifts of healing are manifest so that the Body of Christ may be healthy and care for one another. Jesus instructed us to "heal the sick." (Matthew 10:8). Jesus intended for us as followers of Christ to do as He did. That means we should believe for healing and pray for people for healing. The gift of faith is necessary for this gift to manifest. Mark 16:15 states the following: " they will lay hands on the sick, and they will recover." Some healings are instantaneous and some are gradual. Believe for it and start praying for people to be healed.

The Gift of Working of Miracles

The gift of working of miracles is a two part gift. There is faith for a miracle but also obedience in instruction. An example of this is in John 9. Jesus heals a blind man by spitting on the ground and placing mud in his eyes. He instructs the man to go to the pool of Siloam to be wash his eyes. The man obeyed. The man was completely healed and could see. He had never had vision before so it was pretty awesome to him. He was a living witness of Jesus ability as creator to recreate the eyes so they could see. In Mark 2, Jesus heals a paralyzed man. Jesus commands him to pick up his mat and walk and the man obeys and is completely healed. There is a dynamic of the gift of faith in this gifting but also the obedience to do something that the person could not do before the healing. That is the part of obedience that is an act of faith.

The Gift of Tongues

The gift of tongues usually is giving during the baptism of the Holy Spirit. You are immersed in the Holy Spirit by Jesus Christ. Syllables and words you do not understand will come to you but you must speak them out. It is a heavenly language given by God. It is for you to use in prayer and praise. Sometimes God may use you to speak in tongues during a

Church service so that an interpretation can be give either by you or someone in that meeting.

The Gift of Interpretation of Tongues

The gift of interpretation of tongues is God giving you the understanding or words in English that were spoken in tongues by either you or someone in the church service. The understanding of what your praying is a special blessing because not only are you speaking God's word or praying by the Holy Spirit, but God is giving you understanding in English as well.

The Gift of Prophecy

Often during our church services, the gift of prophecy may come forth. It is a word of exhortation, edification or comfort (1 Corinthians 14: 3). It is giving words to encourage or build up and strengthen the church. Usually, right after the prophetic word people simultaneously begin thanking God and praising Him.

The Gift of Giving

This person usually has an ability to make money or believe for quantities of money to come in to be given for the service of God. The person will feel impressed to give amounts of money to his or her church and other ministries. It includes his or her home church but often reaches to more. For instance missionaries or evangelists or those who are serving in some ministry capacity sharing Christ, preaching or teaching and helping people. The giver is often generous in his or her life also with family, friends and associates. This person knows God gives the money so that it can be used to bless others Deuteronomy 8: 18.

The Gift of Serving

This person is motivated to give of his or her talents and serving abilities which often are very practical such as babysitting or mowing someone's lawn or helping to do a normal task. The person feels a strong desire to help others by serving in practical ways. This is not only in the church but also in people's homes. Sometimes their helpful giving of service leads people to come to know Christ.

The Gift of Encouragement

The gift of encouragement is speaking kind words, encouraging words, words that bring hope or comfort. Usually, a scripture is given but sometimes it is simply comforting words that gives the hearer of those words special peace and encouragement. God moves on the person to speak these words and it is such that the hearer knows God has used the person in some special way, whether or not that person is a Christian.

The Gift of Leading

Rulers or leaders are important because they can show a vision of what the church ought to do. It can mean you are the captain of a sport's team. It can mean you are in a leadership position such as youth leader or teacher. The leader can see a vision of what could be and shares it with the people and they agree and follow him or her. The leader can plan all the details and aspects so it is organized.

The Gift of Mercy

The gift of mercy is feeling what someone else feels. It is a special gift God gives to give us empathy and compassion for others. The person will usually speak a word of encouragement or comfort. Often, the person will pray for the person; it could be short term or may be a long term commitment. Sometimes, they will be drawn together or be in the same place like a class in school where for that duration the mercy can show the love of God to the person causing his or her to know God's deep unconditional love.

These gifts of the Spirit and others mentioned in scripture empower the believer to share truths about Christ with signs and wonders. The people will believe because of the truth spoken and the supernatural manifestation of the gifts. Please pray that God would use you in the gifts of the Spirit in your church and in your school or career or in your social life. God wants to use you. Remember to stir up the gifts of God by praying over yourself literally " I stir up the gift of...." And go through naming each gift. It is worth memorizing them. As you pray stirring them up out loud, faith is released in you to be used by God.

Jesus is the Only Way

Some people believe that God does not give us revelation or insight and that God is trying to stop us from some way in being the best we can be. They believe God wants us to be ignorant. Those people believe the same lie that Satan spoke to Eve in the garden of Eden as he possessed the serpent. He made her believe God was trying to stop them from knowing things and being wise.

Genesis 3: 4 Then the serpent said to the woman, "You surely will not die! 5 For God knows that on the day you eat of it your eyes will be opened and you will be like God, knowing good and evil."

Just the opposite is true. God wants us to go to Him for all wisdom and through the Holy Spirit He can speak to us and give us words of wisdom to speak to people that only God would know. He can give us words of knowledge, things only God knows about. He can use us in interpreting dreams and visions. He can use us – but it is by His Holy Spirit. There is no other way that is true or Holy. God`s way is always superior. In fact God will back His words by sending angels to carry them out. The wisdom God can give to us has these qualities:

True Wisdom

James 3: 17 But the wisdom that is from above is first pure, then peaceable, gentle, open to reason, full of mercy and good fruits, without partiality, and without hypocrisy.

The right way is to go to Jesus and the Holy Spirit will fill you to overflowing. He baptizes us with His Holy Spirit so that we can be empowered for service. He gives us spiritual gifts so we can spread the gospel. That means we are more than able to share Christ because Jesus uses us supernaturally. God gives us wisdom because He is all wise. It surpasses the wisdom of men or of false gods or demons.

Acts 2: 38 Peter said to them, "Repent and be baptized, every one of you, in the name of Jesus Christ for the forgiveness of sins, and you shall receive the gift of the Holy Spirit. 39 For the promise is to you, and to your children, and to all who are far away, as many as the Lord our God will call."

What we have in the new testament is God's indwelling presence. God lives in us and through us. He shows His might through us. He chooses to use us even though He could send angels. He receives glory as we faithfully yield our lives to Him and give ourselves to obey His promptings. Knowing the gifts of the Holy Spirit is essential so that we can pray wisely.

God wants to use you so press into Him in prayer. Make it a priority so that God can quicken you and that you might be full of the Holy Spirit so you can be ready for service.

Prayer

O God I stir up the gifts of the Spirit according to the scripture. I stir the gift of faith. I stir the gift of working of miracles. I stir the gift of healing, I stir the gift of word of wisdom. I stir the gift of word of knowledge and discerning of spirits. I stir the gift of tongues and interpretation of tongues. I stir the gift of prophecy. I stir the gifting of the Holy Spirit. Let them come strong. God use me in the gifts of the Holy Spirit. Use me to communicate Christ. Use me to speak words of faith, hope comfort. Use me to bring healing to people. Use me to shine the light of Christ with my life. Amen.

3 SPHERES OF INFLUENCE

God wants to use us in our spheres of influence. Not many of us will have influence in a king`s palace, but some will. Spheres of influence (Bill Bright and Loren Cunningham, 1995) include government, religion, family, education, media, entertainment, economy, and education. I would add in health care and technology because I believe these are important areas of influence. We do not all have the same spheres of influence. Even though God knew that Babylon was a wicked society, he used Daniel and his friends to protect it and by it save themselves. God gave Daniel and his friends influence in the government of one of the most powerful society on earth even though they were slaves.

God can give you influence in your school, in your use of entertainment or as an entertainer, in education, in family etc. There are people you can connect with that no one else can. Please see that God wants to use you and should you give yourself wholly to God, spirit, soul and body, He will entrust to you the riches of His wisdom.

1 Thessalonians 5: 23 May the very God of peace sanctify you completely. And I pray to God that your whole spirit, soul, and body be preserved blameless unto the coming of our Lord Jesus Christ.

As God gave to Daniel, Hananiah, Mishael, and Azariah wisdom and favour, so will He give to you. Favour is special grace. It is as though you stand out from the crowd. It is as though there a is light upon you that marks you as special. In reality that is exactly what it is. God`s Holy Spirit is living in you and marks you for the kingdom of God. God can cause you to have supernatural favour with people so they will give you special favours or special mercy. You will be the exception. Others may not get the special treatment you receive. God's hand of favour is on you. You may get promtions. You may get moved from regular seating to first class. You may receive special invitations from influential people.

If you do not know what special gifts God has given to you, please get some teaching on Spiritual gifts. Every person who comes to Christ has spiritual gifts. After you are baptized in the Holy Spirit, you become more sensitive to the promptings of the Holy Spirit and God can use you in any or all of those gifts plus others. In my book on Spiritual Gifts I give a survey to help identify your gifts and also an in-depth teaching of the gifts.

and Please find out your spiritual gifts and start using them in the Church. Yes, use your giftings such as tongues and interpretation and prophecy in the local church. It should be a regular part of the Church gathering together.

1 Corinthians 14: 26 How is it then, brothers? When you come together, every one of you has a psalm, a teaching, a tongue, a revelation, and an interpretation. Let all things be done for edification.

Our gathering should be to worship God and so that Spiritual gifts will be released in the church so people can be built up, strengthened, saved, healed, encouraged etc. Please don`t stop there. God wants to anoint you so you can use your spiritual giftings in your school or in your job or in your home or in business etc. God wants you to be a living witness of His glory in whatever sphere of society you are in. God wants to fill you and use you to be light in the earth. That means in your school or job, God wants to place a blessing on you so that others will respect and trust you to pray for them or to speak to them about spiritual matters.

By your godly character and love for God, others can come to know Christ. You may have special privileges in giving wise counsel to people in positions of authority.

Examples of people used to witness the truth of Jehovah God to include Joseph, Nathan the Leper and Daniel. All of these were captives or slaves in foreign countries. All of them God used mightily in those nations.

Joseph

Joseph was a favourite of Jacob because he was the son of Rachel his favourite wife. Jacob made his a multi-coloured beautiful coat to pay honour to him for being a faithful son. His brothers hated him because he was a snitch. He would tell his dad anything his older brothers did that was not right. He was a tattle tale. In spite of this quality, God gave Joseph dreams and revealed things to him about his future through dreams. Joseph didn't know that he shouldn't share it with everyone so he shared it with his whole family.

Genesis 37: 5 Now Joseph dreamed a dream, and when he told it to his brothers, they hated him even more. 6 He said to them, "Please listen to this dream which I have dreamed. 7 We were binding sheaves in the field. All of a sudden my sheaf rose up and stood upright, and your sheaves stood around it and bowed down to my sheaf."

Genesis 37: 9 Then he dreamed another dream and told it to his brothers and said, "I have dreamed another dream. The sun and the moon and eleven stars were bowing to me."

His dreams were about all of his family bowing low before him. His brothers hated him for it. I don't believe for a moment they thought it was a dream from God. They did not know spiritual things. They hated him from jealously and because he always told their dad what wrong things they were doing. They would have killed him but by persuasion of one brother, Reuben, sold him into slavery to Egypt instead. Joseph had every reason to be angry or bitter against his brothers for the rest of his life.

Joseph had the Favour of God on him even in Slavery

An officer of Pharaoh, Potiphar purchased Joseph. Because the hand of God was on Joseph, he had an excellent spirit, Joseph had supernatural favour of God. The favour of God is that undeniable quality about you that shines as a light in the earth. It is the mark of God upon you that causes people to want to treat you special, give you chances no one else gets and give you authority. God gives that person of an excellent spirit, of a pure heart, integrity, passion for God, Holy zeal and excellence in all matters of business as well as in spiritual things.

Genesis 39: 2 The Lord was with Joseph, so that he became a prosperous man. He was in the house of his master, the Egyptian. 3 His master saw that the Lord was with him and that the Lord made all that he did to prosper. 4 Joseph found favor in his sight and served him. So he made him overseer over his house, and all that he had he put under his charge.

Joseph was living in prosperity even though he was a slave. He was given authority and his master agreed that blessing had come to his home after Joseph had come. It would have been very fool hearty and out of character for Joseph to do anything against Potiphar or his family. He had been treated well and given much freedom. Not only was Joseph gifted with how to run things, he was handsome to look upon. His excellence of spirit was interpreted by Potiphar's wife to be an attraction that she lusted after. She threw herself at him and took his garment from him. He escaped that situation immediately and so strongly that he ran naked from the scene. I don't believe he would have told anyone. Potiphar's wife screams in outrage against him for rejecting him and falsely accuses him of trying to rape her.

Potiphar took Joseph and put him in the palace prison. Even though

Joseph was innocent, he was sentenced to prison for a serious crime. Someone accused of such a crime could be put to death. The favour of God was with Joseph even in the prison. The captain of the prison guard saw the favour of God on Joseph and used Joseph's gifts and talents to help things run effectively in the prison.

Genesis 39: 21 But the Lord was with Joseph and showed him mercy and gave him favor in the sight of the keeper of the prison. 22 The keeper of the prison committed all the prisoners that were in the prison to the charge of Joseph. So whatever they did there, he was the one responsible for it. 23 The keeper of the prison did not concern himself with anything that was under Joseph's charge because the Lord was with him. And whatever he did, the Lord made it to prosper.

Even though he ends up in the jail of the palace, Joseph has favour with those who are in the prison. Although he is a slave, he is asked to interpret dreams because of God's anointing on him. Both the cup bearer and the baker of Pharaoh are thrown into prison. Joseph cares for them.

Genesis 40: 2 Pharaoh was angry with his two officials, with the chief of the cupbearers and with the chief of the bakers. 3 So he put them in confinement in the house of the captain of the guard, in the prison, the place where Joseph was confined. 4 The captain of the guard charged Joseph with them, and he attended to them.

While in prison both the cupbearer and the baker have dreams that perplexed them. They tell them to Joseph.

Genesis 40: Then Joseph said to them, "Do not interpretations belong to God? Please tell them to me."

God gives Joseph the interpretation of both of their dreams and asks them to please remember him before Pharaoh. The interpretation of the dreams happens exactly as Joseph had said but the cup bearer soon forgets the kindness of Joseph because he is in comfort living in the palace. After two years pass, Pharaoh has a dream that bothers him. He demands that his wise men interpret the dream for him. The Pharaoh knows there is meaning in the dream because it is repeated but he does not understand the meaning. Finally, as word goes around the palace that Pharaoh demands an interpretation of the dream, the cup bearer remembers Joseph who interpreted his dream.

Genesis 41: 14 So Pharaoh sent and called for Joseph, and they brought him hastily out of the dungeon. He shaved himself, changed his clothes, and came to Pharaoh.

God reveals the meaning of Pharaoh's dream to him through Joseph. There will certainly be 7 years of plenty in Egypt followed by 7 years of famine. Joseph gets the interpretation of the dream and also a word of wisdom about it to give to Pharaoh. Interpreting a dream is more than just giving the meaning; if it is a dream of warning, God gives some solution to remedy the situation. Joseph speaks these words of wisdom, by divine inspiration, to Pharaoh.

Genesis 41: 33 "Now, therefore, let Pharaoh seek out a man who is discerning and wise and set him over the land of Egypt. 34 Let Pharaoh do this, and let him appoint officials over the land and collect the fifth part of the produce of the land of Egypt in the seven abundant years. 35 Let them gather all the food from those good years that come and lay up grain under the authority of Pharaoh, and let them keep food in the cities. 36 This food will be for a reserve for the land for the seven years of famine which will be in the land of Egypt, so that the land does not perish during the famine."

Truly Pharaoh realizes the hand of God by seeing the wisdom of the interpretation and also the wise counsel given by Joseph. Pharaoh, utters these words:

Genesis 41: 39 And Pharaoh said to Joseph, "Since God has shown you all this, there is no one as discerning and wise as you. 40 You will be over my house, and according to your word all my people will be ruled. Only in regard to the throne will I be greater than you."

In an instant, Joseph is raised up from a slave in prison into a place of prominence and favour being second in command in Egypt. He had been taken as a slave. God used him to influence the government of Egypt and to spare Egypt from the famine to come. Because of this, Egypt prospers and Joseph`s brothers come to buy grain because of the severe famine in their land. Joseph forgives his brothers and welcomes them to come live in the land of Goshen. God used one slave, with an excellent spirit, to influence an enemy nation and to save not only all of them but to save his family.

Naaman the Leper's Maid

Naaman the leper's maid was a prisoner taken from her home in Israel. Because of her faith in God, she sowed a Word of hope into the family of the leper. Even though he was a commander and rich and of prominence, his leprosy would have isolated him and given him a rough life. His maid (that he had taken as a slave in battle) spoke words of hope into the family.

2 Kings 5: 2 The Arameans had gone out raiding and had taken captive a little girl from the land of Israel, and she waited on the wife of Naaman. 3 She said to her mistress, "If only my lord were before the prophet who is in Samaria! Then he would take away his leprosy from him."

The maid's statement might have seemed too good to be true but it offered hope. It reached the influence of the throne of the nation as the king sent Naaman with a letter offering money for healing. The offering of money for healing wasn't correct (you never have to pay for God's mercy) but they didn't know how good Jehovah God was. Once he gets to Israel, he sends word to Elisha the prophet with an offer of money. Elisha doesn`t even go in person, he sends a messenger. I`m not sure that we understand that even though Naaman was an enemy of Israel, he was still an important man. It would have been proper for Elisha to greet him with respect and take the gift of money. That would have been the politically correct thing to do. But Elisha the prophet, wasn`t politically correct. He was theologically correct. He obeyed God only. He sent a messenger who simply instructed Naaman to dip himself in the Jordan river 7 times.

Naaman is completely offended. Not only doesn`t Elisha come in person but he gives him a simple solution as though Naaman`s request isn`t considered seriously. That is his perception but the truth is Elisha was getting his instructions from God not from a rule book. Naaman is angry and stubborn. He has been insulted and is about to leave Israel in his pride. One of his servants appeals to him and asks him to do this simple thing. The servant talks wise council to him and Naaman obeys the commandment to dip into the Jordan river. After the 7th dip, he comes up out of the water completely healed and converted to worship God.

2 Kings 5: 15 Then he returned to the man of God, he and all his company. He came and stood before him, and he said, "Now I know that there is no God in all the land, except in Israel. Now take a gift from your servant."

This important man, an enemy, suddenly becomes a believer in Jehovah God because of Elisha, because the servant maid that gave him hope in God. Elisha refuses the money because he is obeying God and because he wants God to get all the glory for healing Naaman. Naaman is so moved to new faith that he asks special mercy upon himself for having to bow in a pagan temple with his master. This is true conversion faith. He realizes only the God of Israel is God.

2 Kings 5: 18 But may the Lord pardon your servant on one account: When my master enters the house of Rimmon to worship, and he leans on my hand, and I bow down in the house of Rimmon, when I do bow down in the house of Rimmon, may the Lord pardon your servant on this one account."

Because of that young maid's boldness to speak hope for healing, Naaman the leper went and was healed. Certainly, he believed in the God who healed him.

God's Spirit Lives in Believer's Today

These examples are in the Old Testament. That doesn't mean that God doesn't give wisdom or interpretation of dreams to day. In fact, God promises the Holy Spirit will be poured out in the latter days.

Joel 2: 28 And it will be that, afterwards,
    I will pour out My Spirit on all flesh;
then your sons and your daughters will prophesy,
    your old men will dream dreams,
    and your young men will see visions.
29 Even on the menservants and maidservants
    in those days I will pour out My Spirit.

God promises to pour out His Spirit. I believe for it in my generation. I believe for it in the generations to come until Jesus returns. I believe God desires to fill us with the Holy Spirit and use us by giving us spiritual gifts and wisdom beyond the wisdom of the earth. Your gifts can make room for you (Proverbs 18: 6). What that means is the special talents and gifts God has given you can give you authority in realms beyond what you can imagine.

God can give you divine connections so that you may be asked to interpret a dream or to give wise counsel or to be used by God in any of the Spiritual gifts to influence all types of people in society. Would you live in integrity and do as God gives you influence to do? You could impact your generation for God. Pray that God would use you: all your education and training, all your talents and giftings that you might glorify God throughout your life. Offer yourself to serve God in your community, in your province or state or region and in your country.

Isaiah 54:
2 Enlarge the place of your tent,
    and let them stretch out the curtains of your habitations;
    spare not,
lengthen your cords,
    and strengthen your stakes.
3 For you shall spread out to the right hand and to the left,
    and your descendants shall inherit the nations
    and make the desolate cities to be inhabited.

God wants to Use You

This scripture is certainly a promise to Israel but it is also a promise to us as we are made a partaker (Jew and Gentile saved by Jesus Christ the Messiah) with Abraham who received the promises of God by faith alone. We have been engrafted into Jesus Christ – made one with Him. We can pray for God to increase our capacity to receive from Him. This includes resources and finances but it also includes spheres of authority. Pray over the spheres of authority of your life and ask God to use you.

The awesome thing about serving God, is that if you serve Him with a pure heart, with a right motive, and an excellent spirit, He will always bless you in ways beyond what you can imagine. If you truly give your life to God, you will influence people. If your motives are not pure, God surely sees this. Give yourself to God. You may share Christ with the poor, the outcasts, the orphans and widows. You may share Christ with your peers and in your career and local church – I believe most of us have this calling of God on our lives. God can use you to influence rulers of our society. You can be a leader in our society affecting multitudes because of your obedience to God. Pray that God may trust you with the riches of Heaven – souls. He can only trust you with eternal things should you give your life completely, wholly consecrated to Him.

Career, Church and Family

God can use your natural gifts and talents whether you are a plumber or a professor. God can use you in all areas of your obedience. Although God can use you without formal education, I highly recommend you get all the education and training you can get. It is tough to get a job that pays above minimum wage without a college diploma or degree. Education and training give us opportunities to those various spheres of influence. I ask you to consider those spheres and determine – write them in a place so you can remember them – of influence you have.

Most of us influence our family, our peers, concerning careers and members of the body of Christ in the local Church. I believe we should pray to be a Godly influence in these spheres. One of the prayers of the Apostle Paul about the building up of the church is as follows:

Ephesians 1: 15 But, speaking the truth in love, we may grow up in all things into Him, who is the head, Christ Himself, 16 from whom the whole body is joined together and connected by every joint and ligament, as every part effectively does its work and grows, building itself up in love.

This prayer is that the Church of Jesus Christ is compared to a physical body, where all parts are together helping each other to function. Should all members of the body of Christ be strengthening the other parts, the Church would be strong and the glory of God would be evident in us as a living organism is distinct from things that have no life such as rocks or earth. You can influence the people in your local church by praying for them as a whole and praying for those in your immediate life. We can pray, bring a psalm or a hymn or a scripture and speak it to the congregation or to our Bible classes. It is a direct way of building up the body of Christ.

People Within the Different Spheres

We should pray over the people we come into contact with in each of these spheres. I see these areas of influence but I also accept them as areas of stewardship. Because we are God's servants, we have authority in all spheres of our lives. It matters that we care and that we pray over the areas of our society we influence. Our actions must be godly and pure. People watch us and will see if we are true to our faith by our deeds. They know if we only talk faith but don't live it. Our prayers release angels into the earth to bring God's will to come to pass. It may mean angels are released to protect or defend someone. It may mean angels fight to release captives. It may mean angels release messengers into areas of society. Prayer is a mighty weapon. Don't ever underestimate the value of your prayers. God is merciful. God may use you to pray for repentance or revival of a sphere of society or for your region.

Sphere of Media

I am praying for God to release people into this sphere. This would include TV anchor people, news writers, producers, reporters, magazine writers, photographers, film crew people – all aspects of media. If you desire for God to use you in this way, please, pray about it and research the best schools to get you the education you need for the job. You may study very specifically at certain colleges or universities so that not only is it your passion, but also you get the best education possible. Media influences what people see, hear, believe, know etc. Media not only reflects culture, it defines it.

Sphere of Entertainment

This sphere is core to the culture of our lives because it is what most people do in their leisure activities. It includes music, art, dance, sculpture, painting, photography, comedy, acting, film directing, producing, writing of books, writing TV series, movies, singing and music, sound and lighting technicians etc. I would include athletes in this sphere because especially in North America we are attracted to sports. Our athletes are excellent and highly paid with much prestige and almost like heroes to children and teens. Should you play an instrument or play a sport, you affecting these spheres of influence for your peers. Should it be your talent and your desire, you could be paid very well to be a part of this sphere. There are multitudes of people who try, but the competition is really high. My recommendation is that you pursue it but also get a post-secondary diploma or degree so that you may also may have practical financial income.

Sphere of Government

Both Canada and the United States became countries because of a strong Judeo- Christian heritage. The reason most people came to North America was for religious freedom as well as other freedoms and those who wanted to be pioneers. Until recently, both Canada and the United States were recorded in official documents as being Christian nations. The laws that first were established were based on the commandments of the Bible. The early government were mostly Christians.

It is essential that those who uphold Christian values and beliefs get into positions of government of all type so that a Christian perspective can be acknowledged. If we want to see our nation change, we must get Christian presidents, prime ministers, mayors, managers, council people etc. should you be interesting in impacting your nation by being involved in government, you must be strong and have a solid support system because there are spiritual barriers you will face as a Christian. God will give you favour and bless you but you must keep your heart pure with Christ as your main strength. Pray that God may raise up righteous, godly government officials who will care about Christian concerns and about turning the tide of our nation to God.

The Sphere of Economy is most serious as it involves what we use on earth as a priority for all types of business transactions – money. This includes business owners and entrepreneurs and business managers and economists. It includes investors and company owners. There are certain business people that become so successful financially that their reputation is such that they give to their communities and regions and invest in the local and regional economy affecting thousands and thousands of people bringing prosperity to the sphere they influence. Usually a diploma, a degree and even a Masters of Business Degree are helpful pursuing this field. You would have to be wise about investing and purchasing and sales and in vision for affecting your region. This is an excellent field to go into to prosper yourself but also to affect your city or province or state. Sometimes, the business men or woman, impact all of North America or even the globe.

The Sphere of Health Care

In Canada, we have an excellent health care system that provides care for all citizens regardless of their financial situation. There are doctors, educators, nurses, lab technicians, technicians for all types of health care machines, dentists, dental hygienists, chiropractors, physiotherapists, specialists etc. in this field.

This field is always in demand, so study opportunities are competitive with only the students with highest grades making it into graduate studies. Those who genuinely love people and helping people can serve in these fields bringing physical aid to people as well as earning a good living. Dedication to studies as a priority, volunteer work, care for the community, good character and excellence are all character qualities of those who are accepted into these fields of study.

The Sphere of Technology

This would include all aspects of science and technology so I would include aerospace designers, specialists, astronauts, computer science people, inventors, biologists, botanists, zoologists, archeologists, highly educated and prominent people who are constantly creating and imagining and exploring with use of computer and other technology to advance our society. These people are sometimes professors who do research but sometimes they are entrepreneurs who are brilliant in certain areas of technology. Education in science and technology and computers is highly recommended for those of you desiring this field.

Prayer

O God, show me the spheres of society I can influence and instruct me so that I can speak words of life into them. God direct my steps and my paths into the career you would have me go into that I would enjoy and could contribute much to, for your glory. Show me how I can most effectively impact my nation during my life through career and other spheres of society that you give me entrance in. Amen.

4 THE LATTER RAIN MOVEMENT

I had the privilege of intimately knowing some of the saints who lived through the Latter Rain Movement of the 1940's and 50's. These people often talked about how it all changed within a day. My friend said that they gathered to pray every day during the second World War for protection and safety of the troops. It was a daily dying to self to pray for others. Even after the war, they still gathered believing for God to move. I am talking about thousands of people who wanted God to move upon the Church of North America with revival. It was all over North America – pockets of people praying for revival.. My friend shared with me the difference a day made. She said she was in deep intercessory prayer weeping and travailing (deep prayer with sobs praying in the Holy Spirit) for revival to come to the nation and literally lying on the floor praying. She said it was although every ounce of her was being poured out in intercessory prayer. She lay prostrate on the altar praying for hours. She felt the Holy Spirit pouring out in intercession for her nation. The very next day, during the church service, something changed that changed everything.

As they sang worship songs and rejoiced in a usual Sunday service, suddenly the Holy Spirit moved in the new song of the LORD. It began in pockets of people within the congregation praising with tongues and some praising in their natural language but all glorifying God in a personal way. It was like a gusher. Praise and worship was bubbling forth from all the congregation. Suddenly, in the church there was the sound of heaven with antiphonal singing and praising and tongues and interpretation of tongues and the gift of prophecy came strong. Revival had come. Their days of prayer that had gone on for years were answered. People would go down to the altar without an altar call to rededicate their lives to God. People would begin sobbing during the worship services as God healed them. Healings, miracles and prophecy were strong gifts active in the church.

It wasn't for a day or a week. It went on and on for over a decade. It was followed by the Healing Movement of the 1960's. People who heard that God was healing people would line up an hour early before church so they could get a spot in line to be prayed for. People would stay late after church to receive prayer. Prophetic praise released people into their giftings. Some gave their lives to be pastors or teachers or missionaries. God used personal prophecy to unlock the secrets of people's hearts setting them free to live for God. People were delivered from addictions to alcohol or drugs or sexual sin.

It didn't happen for no reason. The people desired God more than anything. Thousands of people sought God for revival. There was a nation (the United States) moved to prayer for revival and hope for their society. It spread into Canada. The revival brought life because God was manifesting His presence in the services with outward sign and wonders.

Throughout the revivals of the last 60 years, God has drawn people to pray and intercede, for our nation and for all types of people in our nations and throughout the earth believing for revival and salvation of multitudes.

I have researched and learned from the excellent Teaching Movement of the 1970's that gave us excellent Bible teachers in prominent media coverage such as Kenneth and Gloria Copeland, Kenneth Hagin, Marilyn Hickey and Joyce Meyer. The Charismatic movement of the 1970`s saw the outpouring of the Holy Spirit on the denominations. People desired God so strongly that they prayed and sought God and God poured out his Spirit baptizing people in the Holy Spirit. Excellent leaders well known learned people such as David Duplesis, Derek Prince and Katheryn Coleman, Ralph Martin, were able to minister to Christians of different denominations even though they were baptized in the Holy Spirit speaking in other tongues. They were gentle and not pushy about the Charismata or gifts if the Holy Spirit. They preached openly the baptism of the Holy Spirit and spoke from their experience. There was a desire for a real and living God in the Christian Church of North America. The Roman Catholic Church saw a revival with the baptism of the Holy Spirit in what they termed renewal.

I witnessed Roman Catholic and Anglican nuns who would come to our large church in the evenings especially when we had prayer and fasting and preaching on healing. They wore their habits but freely lifted their hands and voices to praise and worship God in English and in tongues.

During the 1980`s there was a strong Prophetic Movement occurring in the United states especially but also in Canada. Prophets such as Bill Hamon, Rick Joyner, Peter Wagner, Cindy Jacobs, Emmanuel Cannistraci rose to prominence because of their being used by God to prophesy and pray for the United States and other countries. They prayed for all the earth to be filled with the glory of God. They had a vision of global Harvest. They began to speak of global revival. They would speak so that people would give their lives wholly to God.

The Apostolic Movement of the 1990's was a release of church planters and those who could release giftings in people. It is as though those who founded and built churches suddenly saw the need to build and plant churches all over the United States and Canada as well as other countries. They began to reproduce themselves by imparting into their partners and supporters. They mentored people and released them into ministry. These include Peter Wagner, Keith Butler, T. D. Jakes, Bill Hammon, Barbara Yoder, Creflo Dollar, John Wimber and Jenzen Franklyn and others.

Evangelists Necessary

Presently, there is a movement in the North American Church among Apostles and Prophets quite strong. There are pastors and teachers. What I do not see as strong is the ministry gift of Evangelists. It was strong in the 1950`s and 1960`s with Oral Roberts, Kathryn Kuhlman, Rex Humbard and later Benny Hinn. Presently, I believe the Body of Christ requires a loosing of Evangelists who will go preach the gospel throughout North America and the earth. Benny Hinn, Marilyn Hickey and others faithfully hold Crusades overseas as well as preach in North America and Europe. I pray they will impart their vision for global evangelism to this generation.

I truly believe we have not yet seen the fulfillment of God's promise that the knowledge of the LORD would cover the whole earth as the waters cover the sea. I believe God wants to pour out His Spirit on our nation and all the nations.

Habakkuk 2: 14 For the earth will be filled with the knowledge of the glory of the Lord,
    as the waters cover the seas.

The situation of the Church of North America

I am believing for God to pour out a spirit of intercession and supplication upon the Church as never before. As people intercede for their spheres of authority, including their regions and their nation, God and His people become one in prayer. God's desire is for the outpouring of His Spirit on all people. There have been movements of the Holy Spirit in the last decade. There was an outpouring of the Holy Spirit with manifestations of His presence in Brownsville, Toronto and Kansa City. People came from all over the world to get into these services. There were healings, deliverance manifestations of the Holy Spirit and a release of people into ministry because of these meetings. There is a present desire in people for God. There are pockets of revival throughout the United States and in some places in South America and Africa and Asia. I believe God wants to release His Spirit in a dimension we have never known.

What you can do

Pray for the mercy of God for your city, province or state, country. Pray for mercy on us and that God would pour out His Spirit as He promised. The book of Revelation gives us insight to what I believe to be the final outpouring of God's Spirit before the return of Jesus. As Daniel prayed repenting for his nation Israel, let us pray for our nations repenting. Truly as a society we in North America have not followed God in our government or in our secular society.

Canada and the United States were once known as Christian Nations. I pray this will once more be said of us. There is a need for a miracle of governmental shifting for this to occur. We must repent, turn away from covetousness and lusts of the flesh and turn to God. I am generalizing but it is true. Only God can bring such a revival. We can do something about it. We can pray. Each person that prays can release others. As we pray, God releases angels who release answers to prayer.

The Angel with the Everlasting Gospel

Revelation 14: 6 Then I saw another angel flying in the midst of heaven, having the eternal gospel to preach to those who dwell on the earth, to every nation and tribe and tongue and people. 7 He said with a loud voice, "Fear God and give Him glory, for the hour of His judgment has come. Worship Him who made heaven and earth, the sea and the springs of water."

In God's mercy, He has not yet returned. Surely we are closer to the return of Jesus with each passing day, but if people have not known the love of God or the saving or healing grace of God or witnessed His glory, they will remain unchanged. Stewardship over areas of influence means prayer over areas of influence – praying for God to raise up leaders and praying for God to turn our hearts to Him. It means intercession until Jesus comes as He promised He would.

Matthew 24 warns us of wars and plagues and pestilence and Romans tells us of people being so much into sin that they do not honour God in any way. God gives us instruction on how to identify what type of people are around us. It should compel us to pray. The fruit of people is in their doings and in their words.

Matthew 7 16 You will know them by their fruit. Do men gather grapes from thorns, or figs from thistles? 17 Even so, every good tree bears good fruit. But a corrupt tree bears evil fruit. 18 A good tree cannot bear evil fruit, nor can a corrupt tree bear good fruit. 19 Every tree that does not bear good fruit is cut down and thrown into the fire. 20 Therefore, by their fruit you will know them.

May God give us discerning of spirits strong so that we can identify the origin of people who are attracting a following or those who rise into positions of authority.

The Church Should Shine

Isaiah 60 explains that even as the world becomes darker in sin and ignorance of God, the Church of Jesus Christ will shine brighter and brighter. The Church of Jesus Christ will be the stewards of God's manifest presence in our generation. That means wholly giving ourselves to be used by God; we should be people of an excellent spirit so God may use us. As there are areas of influence for each of us, pray that God can use you to intercede and to pray and to be a living witness He can use with the gifts of the Spirit to impact your generation.

Prophetic Word

I am calling you to a level of excellence beyond all your education and gifts and talents. Don't rely on your own self. Don't rely on your education alone. Invite God to use you in your job, in your career, in your social life. In all areas of life that you go, you bring Jesus Christ with you. Pray that Christ would be evident in your life in all spheres of it.

Pray to Align with God

Go to the right source. Go to Jesus. Have nothing to do with horoscopes or false gods or people who say they are Christians but openly sin and do not repent. It's not wrong to want to know spiritual things. It is wrong to go to the wrong source. We were created as spiritual creatures so we desire to know spiritual things. Your desire to know spiritual things is evidence of God drawing you to Himself. He wants the best for you. He will give you the best. No matter what any other way would offer you it can never satisfy you. The only way you can be satisfied and joyful and fulfilled is by going to Jesus Christ. He will release joy, peace, abundance etc. in your life. We do not seek Him for these things but by seeking Him, His presence manifests these things.

Each day commit yourself to God fresh and expect God to use you. Pray that God may use you. He will. But you cannot be living as in the Eon (Greek) or world system and be a vessel for the glory of God. You live in the world, but you are different; to those with an excellent spirit, their eyes are fixed on Jesus. The earthly society we live in is not our true citizenship. Our allegiance is to Jesus Christ and the kingdom of God. It means we are different. It doesn't mean we don't care for sinners. We should care by giving, serving, preaching, but we don't do the same things they do.

Repent for Yourself, for your People and for your Nation

It is an act of human will, praying to be used. It means your life is different. It means like Daniel, you do not partake of the "king's meat". What this is – the king`s bloody meat- is different to each person but if there is anything that you are a part of that you know is not pleasing to God or if you are going to a place you wouldn't bring Jesus with you, stop it. Repent. Stop doing it – turn to God. It means things that may be treasured on earth by thousands of people that are costly and desirable to unsaved people – you keep away from completely. It might mean less TV viewing. It might mean listening to different music. It might mean not going to places where other people are doing drugs or getting drunk. If you could go to those places, even if you are not participating, your presence is consent saying it is ok.

There could be a different teaching on what to do with your life if you're not addicted to social media or sex or drugs or other things. The truth is you may be alone until the right people connect with you or you with them. Should you want to live for God but come from a non-Christian home, you may find inspiration in my book on The High Call of God: a Life Worth Living. God is always faithful. He will always bring someone into your life who you can talk about spiritual things with and pray with. Pray that God would give you godly Christian friends who would encourage you to use your gifts and talents and to live a Holy life for God. Decide to be as Daniel who purposed in his heart to live a godly life. You purpose in your own heart to live a godly life.

Freedom of Choice

In North America we enjoy so many freedoms for which I am truly thankful. Freedom is an awesome thing. Because of it, you and I can pursue any education or training we want. We can choose the career we desire. We can choose to marry or stay single. We can choose our friends. We can express our opinions and vote for people who share our values. Freedom is so important to me. The freedom of being completely set free is the most awesome freedom any person can know.

Neither Joseph, not Naaman the leper's maid or Daniel and his friends were conquered by their captivity. They used their position as slaves to proclaim the glory of God to the people who had taken them captive. They used the authority of heaven to impact the people around them directly affecting the nations they were in. I believe God wants to raise up some faithful people who will not be in any bondage, people who are free because of the blood of Jesus Christ and because each day they offer themselves as a living sacrifice to God (Romans 12: 1-2).

Relying on the Holy Spirit

No matter how much education you may have, your source is higher – God is the ultimate source. God can use all the things you have learned in your life including your education and qualifications to position you in jobs and in situations where he can use you for His glory. There are Christians who are educated – doctors, dentists, professors, teachers, government employees etc. They can use their education to do their jobs but their source is higher.

If you are a born again Christian, you gave your life to Christ. I am saying it isn't enough to only do it once. Do it once and you are saved. There is more to life than assurance you are going to heaven. Offer yourself to God daily as a living sacrifice as the scripture commands us.

Romans 12: 1 I urge you therefore, brothers, by the mercies of God, that you present your bodies as a living sacrifice, holy, and acceptable to God, which is your reasonable service of worship. 2 Do not be conformed to this world, but be transformed by the renewing of your mind, that you may prove what is the good and acceptable and perfect will of God.

I mean each day offer up yourself to God and ask Him to use you that He could be glorified in your life. God can inspire you and quicken things you have learned so that you can solve things other people cannot. God can give you words of wisdom so you will have exactly the right words to speak in tough situations. God can give you words of knowledge so you can speak with authority things God shows you. These could bring people to their knees. God can give you discerning of spirits so keen that you will sense what is compelling the people to speak or act the way they do. The Holy Spirit is the highest authority. Put your hope and your faith in the Holy

Spirit to use you each day with expectation and expect God to give you divine connections.

Each day, ask the Holy Spirit to lead you so that He might use you in your job whether it is truck driver, carpenter, business owner or executive. God wants to use us, the body of Christ - all members- all over the earth in all spheres of society. The thing about God though is He responds to faith. Our presenting of ourselves shows our willingness to obey God and be led by the Holy Spirit. That willingness plus faith and expectation makes us candidates for divine connections.

Hebrews 11: 6 And without faith it is impossible to please God, for he who comes to God must believe that He exists and that He is a rewarder of those who diligently seek Him.

Prayer

O God I give myself to you today and ask you to use me in speaking words of life into people. Holy Spirit, quicken the scriptures to me so that I can speak a living word to people. Engraft the Word of God into my very soul so that I might be a living epistle. I desire to glorify you with my life. Amen.

5 DIVINE CONNECTIONS

Divine connections may come through you simply doing your job with a special moment where God shines through you showing the mercy and compassion of Christ through you to a customer or colleague. It could mean you meet someone who needs something that you have an abundance of. It could mean that you meet someone who is new in town and is looking for a good church. There are endless possibilities because God knows how to use you with all the aspects of your life, job, family life, church, interests etc. so that He can provide for someone who has a need. It is not just one way either. You may meet someone who has the exact skills and talents and influence to connect you with a supply or a resource that is precisely an answer to your prayers.

GIVING

God can use anyone but He is specifically looking for people of an excellent spirit. He wants to be able to promote those who are wholly consecrated to Him. He delights in us and will always bless us more than anything we could ever do or give to others. You may have heard the saying You cannot out give God. It is so true. No matter how much you invest in others, no matter how much you give of yourself, your resources or your time – God will always bless you with more than enough.

2 Chronicles 9: 9 For the eyes of the Lord move about on all the earth to strengthen the heart that is completely toward Him.

God's gifts or blessings to us most often does not come from the same person we gave to. In fact, He especially blesses us for giving to those who could never repay us. God wants to bless you with health and long life. We know this because of scriptures:

Psalm 91: With long life I will satisfy him
and show him My salvation.

God's Word tells us He does. God wants to prosper you financially, physically and spiritually.

Psalm 103: 2 Bless the Lord, O my soul,
and forget not all His benefits,
3 who forgives all your iniquities,
who heals all your diseases,

4 who redeems your life from the pit,
   who crowns you with lovingkindness and tender mercies,
5 who satisfies your mouth with good things,
   so that your youth is renewed like the eagle's.

In Deuteronomy 28, God declares His heart towards us. If you haven't read this scripture recently, read it and realize that because of Jesus Christ, these blessings apply to us as Christians. They apply to you personally. God delights in blessing us or giving to us as a parent delights in giving gifts to his or her children. God's goodness towards us is not an excuse to slack off on anything. We should desire to be excellent in what we do for God. We should live all parts of our lives as giving to God. This means a right heart attitude. It means a desire to give the best and do the best. It means caring and concern for people. It means we are living sacrifices. It is our desire to live for God continuously day after day, all the days of our lives.

Real Christians

Christians of an excellent spirit, true in all their ways, showing the love of God and mercy of God in practical ways expressing the scriptures with their very lives. They have the anointing of the Holy Spirit on them so strong, they encourage you just by you being with them. Did you ever know people like this? I have been privileged to know many. They are the same way in the pulpit or in their ministry as they are in their private lives or their leisure lives. Truly, godly character is the evidence of Christ in their lives. They don't lead a double life. They live radically for Christ. They will not compromise God's Word. They align their lives with God's Word. They live what they believe. People who are Christians respect them but there are non-Christians that will respect them because of their excellence in both skills and attitude.

God Cares about all Creatures

God has used me to be a divine connections for both animals and people. I understand some Christians will not understand that God truly cares for every animal and how we treat them. But it is true. I know this because has put within my heart special love and compassion for animals. The same prompting of the Holy Spirit that moves me to help people, causes me to rescue and care for animals. Throughout my life, I have been in places where an animal was alone, out of habitat and requiring help. I know it is not a coincidence. I believe should you also have a kind heart towards animals you should do all you can do to help them. Not all people have this same feeling of stewardship for the animals although it is truly what we humans are. Usually people who are kind to animals are also kind to people and vice versa. God is the creator of all and by respecting life, we are wise stewards of what God has put within our care.

Proverbs 12: 10 A righteous man regards the life of his animal, (a)

Pet Shop

During my studies for ministry, often God used me throughout the day to speak to people and to pray for people etc. After one of my ministry classes, I was driving home with a class mate and he asked to stop so he could buy Valentines. I stopped for him. I could have waited in the car or gone in with him. I felt a prompting to go into the pet shop in the same strip mall. Although I love animals, the prompting was unusual because I did not need anything and usually seeing animals in cages is not my favourite thing. I went in and began to look at things that I might buy for my pets and I saw a woman and her daughter. I felt a strong tug at my heart and God speaking to me to go speak to that woman and tell her that God loved her.

Please notice, only minutes ago in minister's training class I had been praying with my whole heart "O God use me!" God was directly speaking to me but I was speaking to Him – I was making excuses. God I do not even know this woman. I do not know what to do. I recognized God's prompting, so I sort of started following her around the store. She was with her daughter and they were looking at purchasing a dog. I tried to come up with clever introductions but did not. I should have been praying and obeying. About 20 or 30 minutes later, the two women were in line to purchase a dog. I bought some insignificant thing. I was in line behind them. As they rang in their purchase, I finally made conversation commenting on the dog. I saw the weak eyes of the older woman and I knew I must speak those words to her.

I spoke and said "God really cares about you. God hears your prayers." If not the exact words, they are of the exact sentiment. I believe God gave me the words as I opened my mouth in obedience. The woman got all teary eyed and confessed she had been praying but did not know if God was listening. The reason for the dog was as a companion for her because her husband of many years had just died. I felt like an idiot for not obeying God as soon as He prompted me. Just because I do not understand does not mean that I should not do it. I believe my words brought some type of comfort to the woman. I went home and prayed for her and repented for not obeying God more quickly.

Luke 12: 12 For the Holy Spirit will teach you at that time what you should say."

Some divine connections are for a once only appearance. Some divine connections lead us to our best friends. Other divine connections can spring us to a new level of life. God can use the ordinary to use us in extraordinary ways. Believe God for and pray for divine connections and favour that will give you opportunities to share Christ with others.

Testimony of Shining as a Fastball Player

I played sports most of my life. I was saved at the age of 22, so in my 20's and 30's, especially, I played sports with excellence and with a desire to give God glory. At first, I still played for my bar teams. I did it because the skill level was high. I played fastball and I could play several positions. I liked to play outfield and I liked to back catch. The competition was high in the league I was in. I played on a travel team. That was my favourite of all teams I played on because I had such an excellent coach. I was somewhat of the dump for jokes about 'Holy Rollers and saints' because I was not drinking alcohol with them.

I would still go to the sports' bar with them because we were sponsored and it was a way of the team celebrating together, but I would drink a pop or order food. Please know, before I was a Christian I engaged in the beer chugging contests these women and teens were doing. I could boast that I could drink more than others and hold my liquor. Sometimes, people would by me drinks to see how much I could hold. The women on my team didn't know this and my coach, who I highly respected for her knowledge of the game and ability to see my strengths and help me to develop them, spoke to me about trying some alcohol.

I shared with her how I had been a drunkard engaging in drinking competitions for before I had become a Christian, but that my faith in God was most important now and I wanted to honour God by not setting a poor example. Even though I shared those words with her, I do not know if she understood. I was living a Christian life and playing competitive fast ball. I got teased and mocked but when I hit a home run, they cheered me on and when I caught a ball or tagged someone out at the plate, the whole team congratulated me. My point is that my talents and skills made it so that even though they didn't like me because I was a Christian, they couldn't talk negative about my ball playing. I received the most sportsman like player award from that team. I highly cherished it knowing that for it to happen, even though they didn't like me as a Christian, they respected me as a player.

Intercessor

You can use your leisure life, your interests, your hobbies and volunteer work to shine the light of Christ. It isn't always easy to be the brunt of jokes about Christians, but I do know that if they have a need they will come to you for prayer. They will see you as a point of connection with God. To people who do not know God, God is scary. Most unsaved people know they are unworthy of God's company. They know they do things that are not right, but they don't know any other way. They fear God but want Him simultaneously. The fear causes them not to pursue God. I would compare this to how God separated Moses and Aaron and the Levites from the rest of Israel at Mount Zion.

Exodus 19: 12 You shall set boundaries for the people all around, saying, 'Take heed to yourselves so that you not go up onto the mountain or touch its border. Whoever touches the mountain will surely be put to death. 13 No hand will touch him, but he shall surely be stoned or shot through, whether it be beast or man. He shall not live.' When the trumpet sounds a long blast, they shall come up to the mountain."

Moses was a prophet but also an intercessor. He would often plead mercy to God for the people of Israel. He would warn the people to revere and honour God and to obey Him. He was an intercessor. God can use you to intercede for others. Because of our sports or our similar interests to others, unsaved people will feel safe approaching us to ask for prayer. Even in their jesting with us mocking us for our faith, they partly know there is some quality about us that makes us different. They might believe it is what we do or don't do but as they can come to know us they will realize it is Who we know, not what we do or don't do. Knowing God intimately gives us boldness to speak for God.

Exodus

Moses did not have the confidence that he could obey God by going to Egypt and demanding that Pharaoh let the Israelites go free. He had been a shepherd in Midian for 40 years and did not believe he was a good speaker.

Exodus 3: 11 Moses said to God, "Who am I that I should go to Pharaoh and that I should bring forth the children of Israel out of Egypt?"

12 And He said, "Certainly I will be with you, and this will be a sign to you, that I have sent you: When you have brought forth the people out of Egypt, all of you shall serve God on this mountain."

God's promise that He would go with him and also that Aaron could help him convinced Moses to go to Egypt. During his 40 year ministry to the Israelites as they were led through the wilderness by God, God imparted His love for Israel to Moses so that Moses would pray and intercede for Israel caring for them as God Himself would.

The Christian life is such that daily we are given the opportunity to choose God first and foremost. God draws you to Himself as a magnet draws iron particles to itself. In the same way, we can yield to God and come to know Him more. There may be some defining moment in your life where you believe you must do something – take a step of faith. To some it could mean studying for ministry or starting a business. To others it could mean rededicating your life to Christ or attending special training. God will direct you personally and let you know also.

Studying for Ministry

More than twenty years ago, I made a serious commitment decision. I decided to study for Minister's training. This meant travelling an hour to and an hour from the church I was attending. The training included a promise to attend both Sunday AM and PM services, being active in the Church, and training classes that filled my calendar so the only day I didn't have school was Friday evenings. I had a job teaching and instructing but it was a job without homework. Ah, it was an excellent job and an excellent fit for my destiny decision to study for ministry.

Often, I would go through a drive thru and eat my supper on the way to Church. I lived that way for about 3 almost 4 years. It was one of the toughest things on me concerning my efforts- mostly because of travel through an International border to get to classes at church. That decision shaped the rest of my life. I only did sports leisurely because of my schedule. I saw less of my family and any friends who were not studying with me. It was a destiny decision. I wanted more of God and nothing else was as important to me.

I knew the Pastor of that Church and the teachers had something to impart to me and I wanted it more than anything. I wanted to be trained to minster to others. I wanted to be trained to train others. I do not regret one of those days I sat in traffic on the highway going to or coming home from church. Every moment brought insight and joy to my life. I had to study for and write exams. I felt the favour of God on me and I experienced it. I was working full time and studying for ministry and volunteering nearly 20 hours a week. I thank God for every minute of it.

Prayer

O God, I feel you drawing me to yourself. I believe you want to use me. Bring me to the place I should be with the right people. Bring me to a place where I can learn about you and be trained to minister to others. Help me clearly see what gifts and talents you want me to use and develop so that I can reach more people for Christ. Amen.

6 COMMITMENT WILL LEAD YOU TO EVANGELIZE

Seasons of Life – Season of Evangelism

During those years of minister's trianing, I knew the favour of God for evangelizing so strong that whether I was in church, or in a restaurant or in a bank or in a grocery store, I had favour to share spiritual things with people. I spoke with many people about the LORD. I had people recommitting their lives to God as well as giving their lives to God. Some people I only saw once; others I adopted and helped find local churches for them to attend. I see those years as golden in terms of their value. I was learning so much and applying it directly with people I was meeting. God's hand of favour was on me. I know that if God can use me, He can use you. Part of it means a commitment to God. I'm not saying everyone has to study for ministry, but in some way, you must make a decision to live wholly for God. The most rewarding, exciting life for you is on the other side of that decision. There are people that you would have opportunity to impact on the other side of that decision. It is boldness for Christ.

Position

Position can give you more opportunities to minister for Christ. It does not mean it is more important than other people but it gives you a place of reaching more people. The sphere is larger meaning you could impact those who know who you are. They do not even have to like you; they just have to know who you are. If people find out you are a celebrity and a Christian, they will scrutinize your life. The world has contempt for Christians and delights in pointing out any weaknesses or faults in people so they can make Christians appear to be weak or untrue. It is certainly true that a higher level or fame, gives people a higher platform for ministry opportunities.

There are sports heroes, famous singers and actors and people who use their fame to give Jesus glory. God blessed them with the most awesome job they dreamed of and they give Him the glory. God provided for them financially more than most people can imagine and they honour Jesus Christ publicly. Some of them travel and speak to youth who might never listen if it were not for the fame and sports or musical talents of the person. If they can give the glory, we certainly should also. Your position can be a platform to share Christ. These people always encourage me because I know they know their source isn't the money or the job or the prestige. They realize Jesus Christ is their source and they use their positions as heroes to share Christ with others. Listen if these people can use their positons to honour God, so should we who are teachers, or clerks or secretaries or delivery people God wants to use all of us not only the rich and famous. Realize that as you share Christ, you are shining the light of the gospel in your sphere of authority.

The Main Thing

Our jobs and success are not the main goals of our lives. Yes, God wants us to be excellent And yes, God wants to use us in all we do. The main reason we live on earth as Christians is to shine the love of Christ into the earth. We are the people God will use to bring Christ to our generation. The purpose for our life is to live for Christ and to be a constant living witness of His resurrection life. Accepting Jesus is more than getting a way to go to Heaven. Accepting Jesus, at some point will give you the choices of growing more as a Christian, seeking God with all your being or not. The more you press in to God, the more you are going to want to share God with others. You don't share Christ because you have to. You share Christ because you realize He is the only way and you care about people so you tell them about God.

Romans 10: 14 How then shall they call on Him in whom they have not believed? And how shall they believe in Him of whom they have not heard? And how shall they hear without a preacher? 15 And how shall they preach unless they are sent? As it is written: "How beautiful are the feet of those who preach the gospel of peace, who bring good news of good things!"[g]

God Uses People

Although God could send angels to speak to people, and sometimes He does, He mostly uses the Church of God on the earth. We are living on the earth as agents of righteousness. God has entrusted to us to be co-labourers with Him so that by the prompting and leading of the Holy Spirit, we might lead others to Christ, or get them to return to Christ. We are as intercessors in prayer and in actions so that those who must know God and are in a position to come to God might be born again. God uses us to be agents of righteousness with Him in eternal matters. Nothing is more satisfying as helping someone to know God and that He truly loves and cares for him or her.

2 Corinthians 5: 18 All this is from God, who has reconciled us to Himself

through Jesus Christ and has given to us the ministry of reconciliation, 19 that is, that God was in Christ reconciling the world to Himself, not counting their sins against them, and has entrusted to us the message of reconciliation.

Giving the Gospel

We should be sowing into the gospel in some way. It can be by loving people one by one. It can be through our jobs and our influence. It can be through our prayers. It can be by giving financially to those who bring the gospel of Jesus Christ to those in other nations. These words were given to the disciples. They are given to us.

Mark 16: 15 He said to them, "Go into all the world, and preach the gospel to every creature. 16 He who believes and is baptized will be saved. But he who does not believe will be condemned. 17 These signs will accompany those who believe: In My name they will cast out demons; they will speak with new tongues; 18 they will take up serpents; if they drink any deadly thing, it will not hurt them; they will lay hands on the sick, and they will recover."

The Commission

Jesus commanded that we Go preach the gospel to every nation, to all people groups of the earth (Matthew 28: 19-20). We must accept this word to us as it not only applies to some Christians but all of us. Some people go on short term missions and some on longer ones. Some of us give financially to those who go on missionary trips. Others support missions through their local church. Pray and truly let God show you where you can serve or give best.

Our mandate as Christians is to give to the gospel. It means giving our lives, our time, our efforts, our finances, our prayers etc. The prime directive of the Church is that the gospel shall be preached to all people groups in every nation. God can and will use us. Some of us may have opportunity to go overseas or to other communities to share Christ. There are some Christian business owners and executives that do business but also privately share Christ as they travel the world. Some may go for one day or a week end. Some may pass out tracts to people. I knew an elderly woman whose passion for God burned so strongly, she carried tracts with her and gave them to people to share Christ. It could mean praying for missionaries. It could mean giving to those who do go. It is the reason we the Church are on the earth. Oh. Never believe there is nothing you have to give. You are a Christian; you have something to give – knowing Jesus Christ is something we can always give. It could be a song. It could be a hug with kind words. As long as you live, there is some aspect of your life you can use to preach Christ with.

Even if it is someone you only see once a week, speak words of encouragement. You can be speaking the scriptures by paraphrasing them so God's word reaches their hearts. Speak words of life. God's Word never returns void. If we sow the Word of God into people, they will respond. Pray for God to quicken you as you speak with various people. God can give you exact words to speak. God can quicken a Word that you speak that releases the person in faith for something.

The amazing thing about God is that He can do this and we might not understand the significance of it until much later. Often God has used me to speak words to people and much later I found out that it impacted them because it encouraged them. I believe God uses us as earthen vessels so He would receive all the glory. None of us could boast. The words come from God. The love comes from God. The glory is all God's.

2 Corinthians 4: 7 But we have this treasure in earthen vessels, the excellency of the power being from God and not from ourselves

Words

The words we speak can bring life or death to a person. We must be wise with our words sowing the word of God into people or sharing God's word in our paraphrase. Harsh words are as arrows that can pierce a person's heart (Proverbs 18:21). Kind words can impart hope and release faith and inspiration. We should pray for God to set a guard over our mouths so that the Holy Spirit will correct us should we say something that does not line up with God's word (Psalm 141:3).

Proverbs 15: 23 A man has joy by the answer of his mouth,
    and a word spoken in due season, how good it is!

What we say to others matters. What we say to ourselves matters. What we say to God matters. The Word of God aligns us with the right words – with right heart attitudes. Pray asking the Holy Spirit to correct you should you be speaking negative words, or words that do not glorify God. The Holy Spirit will do it. You will feel a check in your spirit letting you know it isn't ok. You should repent – ask God to forgive you and speak a word of encouragement or wisdom. Pray that God would give you words to speak.

Words that Bring Encouragement

In the secular world, not many share encouraging words. Often people complain or make jokes about how many days until the week end. The truth is we could share words that encourage, that build up, that add value to a person, that shows respect for a person, that causes that person to be a little brighter and lighter than we first met him or her. Words are like arrows. Some can shoot arrows that are poisonous and cause death and destruction. Others can be words that release joy, peace, faith. Our mouths can make the biggest difference in our jobs, in our sports teams, in our relationships. God gives us the chance to speak life into people. It is so important what we say to people.

I am especially concerned about this because I am a teacher. God lets me know that words of encouragement can cause students to give their best. Words from authority figures can also be as poisonous darts. I have experienced words from teachers that caused me to believe the lie that I could not learn something. People in positions of authority can influence others by their words. How important are the words we sow into people's lives! Literally pray over yourself the scripture:

Psalm 19: 14 Let the words of my mouth and the meditation of my heart
   be acceptable in Your sight,
   O Lord, my strength and my Redeemer.

Ask God to help you. Don't use insults as a joke. Some people jokingly insult each other as though it is all in fun. Words that insult tear down and destroy. Words that are positive release energy and faith and light. Keep a positive attitude – being positive that God can not only use you but that God can use you to share with others – there is always hope. There is always an answer. God is higher than anything. These words are as life boats to people in a world where not many share positive hopes. Most of the news on TV or newspaper reports crimes and war and conflicts. We can be bearers of the good news. There is always a way with God.

As a teacher, I usually encourage students to try their best that they can achieve whatever they set their hearts to accomplish. The truth is most people who make decisions about their life and write these goals down, live to accomplish them. Those who never write their goals and visions, seldom accomplish them. There is a negative sort of viewpoint that directs people saying – you win some, you lose some. Life's not fair. It's tough etc. It's said almost as a joke. It does not in any way encourage or build up anyone.

We should be people sowing words of hope – you can achieve your goals. You can accomplish your dreams. Especially, we who live in North America have been given so much freedom of choice. We can use our freedom to pursue our dreams. Sowing the word of God into people is like giving them a shot of encouragement or a dose of joy or faith. We are dispensers of God's glory. What we say to people can cause them to believe or to hope or to seek God. It matters what we say.

Pray over yourself that you won't use criticism or grumbling or complaining in your life. Instead you will pray to see it as God sees it as an opportunity for you to make a difference. Speak hope to those who are in need of a miracle because we know our God is able to do miracles. We know that Jesus defeated death, hell and the grave and that He rose from the dead and ascended up into heaven. He promised to return. We have hope. We who are Christians realize that even death is not the end. Jesus is eternal life. Knowing God is eternal life. We should encourage ourselves with these words but also others.

1 Thessalonians 4:16 For the Lord Himself will descend from heaven with a shout, with the voice of the archangel, and with the trumpet call of God. And the dead in Christ will rise first. 17 Then we who are alive and remain shall be caught up together with them in the clouds to meet the Lord in the air. And so we shall be forever with the Lord. 18 Therefore comfort one another with these words.

Encourage Yourself in the LORD

Christians can choose to encourage themselves in the LORD and we should. We should do it not only for our own joy but so that we can speak words of life into those people around us. You can speak hope and faith into people's lives that had their heart ripped out of them by tragedy. You can speak encouragement to give hope for a future to someone who has lived through a divorce or the loss of a loved one. It's the words of our mouth that can inspire hope and faith. It's our kind actions to show genuine love and concern by bringing someone a gift or a meal. These things we should do, not because someone asks us but because we live for God and love people. If we truly do love God, we will truly love people.

A Reason for your Life

Please see it wasn't for no reason that God gave Daniel the ability to interpret dreams. God gave him this special ability because He knew Daniel would be in Babylon and could speak it to the King. God used Daniel and his friends to impact Nebuchadnezzar's life. It means God not only cared for those Israelis but also for the king of Babylon. God had a message for him even though he wasn't serving God. Sometimes, God will put you in a place where you will have influence – divine wisdom or knowledge or discernment and there will be others there who have human wisdom or skill or astrology or some other means. They might not be able to give a correct interpretation or give the true situation as it is, but God can use you as the Christian source.

God can speak to you and it can influence all the people in that place as you speak God's wisdom for a solution. God may use you to speak to presidents and kings. You have got to be humble, honest not self-seeking, truthful and desirous to give God glory – of an excellent spirit. God will use you because of your career position or your every day activities. It is so important that our hearts be pure so God can entrust to us the riches of Heaven – speaking God's word to people who lead and govern on earth. You will speak the word because it is the right word to speak not because of selfish gain.

Nebuchadnezzar not only wanted the interpretation for his dream but also wanted the wise men to tell him his own dream. All of the magicians and astrologers could not. Daniel could not except that God revealed it to him. Daniel spoke with such insight and precision, the king could hardly believe it. It was as though he knew only God could know what he had dreamed and what it meant. Because of the interpretation, Daniel was promoted the head of the wise people. You may be the only Christian in your work or school situation, but you could have the favour of God on you to speak words that solve problems or speak encouragement or know the exact solution to a situation.

Daniel 2:

Choose to be a person of an excellent spirit. Decide to live wholly unto God. Give yourself as a daily offering so that God can and will use you in your workplace or school or any place you go. Remember how God used Joseph – even as a slave in a prison, God used him with special interpretation of dreams to bring him to a place of honour in Egypt. From a slave in prison, to the 2nd in command in Egypt, God brought Joseph to a high place of authority. No matter what your position is in society, God can use you.

Pursue your God Given Dreams

If you have not thought about what your biggest dreams to accomplish are, I would highly recommend you being to imagine what would you want to do that you would enjoy more than anything else that you could be glorifying God doing it. Ask yourself how you could most contribute to your society? What would you enjoy doing that you are good at that could glorify God? It could be a ministry position but please know it could also be in any of the spheres of society. Each person has a unique combination of gifts and talents that God has given to use in all spheres of society.

Dream Big. Believe that God can give you a career that you will enjoy so much that you would do it even if you were not paid. The awesome thing is God can give it to you and also financially prosper you simultaneously.

There is no social position where God cannot and will not use you. Whether you are a director or actor or garbage collector or musician. God uses His people in all aspects of life. Whatever realm you are in, whatever spheres of society you influence, use your life to be a living, willing sacrifice – a servant of God – a co labourer with God. Purpose in your heart to wholly consecrate yourself to God so that He can use you. Believe and expect God to use you in the market place. Believe that God will use you in making a difference in your school, your career, your community etc. Be wise so that God can use you throughout all your life. You don't have to be blazing speaking in tongues at your job for God to use you. You don't have to always say 'thus sayeth the Lord' unless God prompts you to. God can use you over the course of your life to be as a light in that place of your business.

Matthew 10: 16 "Look, I am sending you out as sheep in the midst of wolves. Therefore, be wise as serpents and harmless as doves.

You can be a Christian with wisdom, discernment and the prompting of the Holy Spirit to be excellent, to be diligent, to be prudent, to be wise. You can with godly character and lifestyle impact the community around you. If you live in a democracy, as in Canada or the United States, you have so many freedoms and so much opportunity to serve God. Daniel and Hananiah, Azariah, Mishael were taken into captivity and made slaves, yet they used this opportunity to honour God by consecrating themselves wholly. There honouring of the LORD gave them favour with God and in their situation so they were promoted to high positions. God did it for them, He can do it for you. God can use you. Give yourself to Him expecting Him to present you with opportunities to make a difference – divine connections that Jesus Christ may be glorified.

Prayer,

O God, I want to commit myself to you afresh. I want to serve you with all parts of my life. I choose the excellent way. Help me to develop my gifts and talents. Show me how to serve in the body of Christ. Direct my steps in a career path. Give me divine connections. Fill me with your Spirit with wisdom and knowledge and understanding. Give me direction in all aspects of life. I want your best for my life. I want to give you my best. Let me be a person of excellence in all areas of my life that you might receive all the glory. Thank you for filling me and using me. In Jesus name, Amen.

7 CONCLUSION

Dream Big. Realize that God made you because He delights in you. He loves you and gave you special talents, gifts and desires. As long as you are pursuing God first in your life, He wants to bless you financially, physically etc.

John 14: 13 I will do whatever you ask in My name, that the Father may be glorified in the Son. 14 If you ask anything in My name, I will do it.

Of course I am talking about following God with all your heart, being of an excellent spirit. Should this be true, God will cause your life to be blessed in such a way that there are divine connections and you are enjoying your life and reaching people in your career and in your church.

Choose to be Excellent

Live each day giving your best effort at school, at work or with friends. Learn all you can and aim for excellence. I am not only talking about in public. Even in your private life, all that you do, do it as unto God that He would receive glory. In your relationships, in your devotional life, in your hobbies, in your leisure, do something that gives God glory. Remember to thank Him throughout the day. Commune with God. Expect Him to use you. Expect Him to teach you.

Choose friendships that honour God. Only let close to you those who want the best for you and who will build you up and encourage you in Christ.

Colossians 3: 17 And whatever you do in word or deed, do all in the name of the Lord Jesus, giving thanks to God the Father through Him.
Invest in others

The things God has taught you, invest into others. This could mean training someone or it could mean sharing with family or friends. Impart with words but also in prayer.

1 Timothy 4: 14 Do not neglect the gift that is in you, which was given to you by prophecy, with the laying on of hands by the elders.

Devotion

Your devotion to God should include prayer and praise or worship. You should commune with God every day. Making it a priority will mean you are strengthened by God to do everything else in your life. You may get a scripture come to you that will give you the key to your day. Sometimes God has quickened one scripture to me that not only strengthened me but helped me throughout the day to encourage different people.

Keep your relationship with God as you would schedule a meeting with a most important person. The Holy Spirit is the most important person and He can give you insight and wisdom plus joy and rejoicing like no other person could. Book your schedule with God and keep it sacred.

Use a Calendar or an Agenda

Use a schedule or an agenda. Schedule your day. Don't just do nothing. Plan on doing things to build up yourself in your faith. Read an encouraging book or listen to inspirational teaching.

Try to learn something new every day. I don't just mean in school. I mean give yourself to some aspect of learning with excellence. It can be a musical instrument, a sport activity, a new language, a special hobby. By you being the best possible that you can be, you glorify God.

Set Goals for yourself

Recent books I've been reading by John Maxwell and Joyce Meyer have been on the topic of leadership and accomplishing goals. I highly recommend you do some reading of these authors as they have encouraged me to aim for excellence. There are leadership and excellence books on both of their websites. I'm sure there are other worthy leadership teachers, but I mention these because they have impacted me.

Set some short term goals – for a week, a month, 3 months, 6 months a year. Plan what you would like to accomplish in these periods. If you are a student, put your graduation as a goal. It is the start of a new phase of your life. Should you be learning something such as a new language, book your schedule so that each day you accomplish a part of a goal.

Living life on purpose will help you to accomplish more and also to do more. If you want some unscheduled time to either hang out with friends or relax watching TV or movies etc., book a spot for it where you can do whatever you want that day or those hours. Don't let yourself get in the habit of video games all day. I know it is fun but you should master your schedule to be a person of excellence. I believe this is for all people not just teens or students.

In Light of Eternity

You should be enjoying your life. You should be excited about each day and the opportunities God gives each day. God wants you to be joyful and do things that not only give you pleasure but give Him glory. That includes finding out what you are good at and developing those talents and gifts. It includes doing your best in school, giving your best effort. It includes connecting with other people of faith and worshipping, praising, serving and giving to honour God. Pray for God to give you divine perspective. What it will do is cause you to thank God for each moment on earth but also remind you that this life is temporary. It will cause you to care about the present so you can make a difference in your society. It will also cause you to be merciful caring for those who do not know Christ.

Ephesians 2: 4 But God, being rich in mercy, because of His great love with which He loved us, 5 even when we were dead in sins, made us alive together with Christ (by grace you have been saved), 6 and He raised us up and seated us together in the heavenly places in Christ Jesus, 7 so that in the coming ages He might show the surpassing riches of His grace in kindness toward us in Christ Jesus.

Prayer

I pray that God quicken you to realize His deep love for you beyond what you have known (the height, the width the depth the breadth Ephesians 3: 18). May God use your desire to live for Him to teach you about yourself, your gifts and talents. May God cause you to develop those gifts and talents and use them to find a career that you will enjoy and that will affect many people. May God use you to minister to people spirit to spirit, giving your best and expecting God to use you. The words you say, the things you do, the gifts you give, may they bring glory to Christ and much joy to you. Amen.

Receive it as a prayer for you because I am writing this book to minister to you.

OTHER BOOKS BY CHRIS A. LEGEBOW

Available on Amazon.ca Amazon.com or Amazon.ca or Kindle
Or the Create Space webstore.

2016

Discovering and Using your Spiritual Gifts. Living Word. 2016.

Kinds of Prayer. Knowing Them and Using Them Effectively: Living Word. 2016.

Living Life Fully: Knowing your Purpose. Living Word. 2016.

The High Calling: Life Worth Living. Living Word. 2016.

2017

An Excellent Spirit: Living Life Wholly Unto God. Living Word. 2017.

The Anointing: the Glory of God. Living Word. 2017.

ABOUT THE AUTHOR

Chris Legebow is a Christian Professor of English and Communications. She has taught at the elementary, high school and College and University levels. She has ministered in her local churches in intercessory prayer, teaching Sunday school and other Christian Doctrine classes to children and youths. She has preached to congregations and given her testimony. Although she was not raised in a Christian home, she came to know Jesus Christ as her Saviour and LORD while she was studying in University. This radically transformed her life in terms of priorities and commitment.
She has a strong passion for the great commission – that Jesus Christ would be preached throughout all the earth believing that it a major sign of the LORD's return. She has been a part of several different types of full gospel charismatic churches but has also gained much of her insight and enlightenment from Christian Media and broadcasting. She hopes to continue ministering, serving, interceding and giving and teaching until the LORD returns.